What's in this book

学习内容 Contents		2
读一读 Read		4
听听说说 Listen and say		12
写一写 Write		16
多元学习 Connections		18
温习 Checkpoint		20
分享 Sharing		22

This book belongs to _____

中秋节 Mid-Autumn Festival

学习内容 Contents

沟通 Communication

称呼家庭成员
Address extended family members

生词 New words

- ★ 外公　　mother's father
- ★ 外婆　　mother's mother
- ★ 来　　　to come
- ★ 休息　　to rest
- ★ 老　　　old
- ★ 哭　　　to cry
- ★ 笑　　　to laugh
- 舅舅　　mother's brother
- 阿姨　　mother's sister
- 叔叔　　father's younger brother
- 姑姑　　father's sister
- 电话　　telephone
- 喂　　　hello (when answering the phone)

句式 Sentence patterns

舅舅和阿姨也来了。
My mother's brother and sister also came.

叔叔和姑姑没来。
My father's younger brother and sister did not come.

跨学科学习 Project

认识全球受欢迎的节日
Learn about the popular festivals around the world

文化 Cultures

庆祝中秋节的方式
Mid-Autumn Festival celebrations

Get ready

1. How often do you see a full moon?
2. Have you heard of the Mid-Autumn Festival?
3. Do you know what people do at the Mid-Autumn Festival?

今年中秋节,外公、外婆在我家。舅舅和阿姨也来了。

我们在花园里吃月饼和水果。天上的月亮圆圆的。

爷爷、奶奶、叔叔、姑姑没来,他们去中国旅行了。

他们的中秋节怎么样呢？我和爸爸给他们打电话："喂，……"

九点半,外公、外婆回卧室了,因为老人要早点休息。

大家看着我和姐姐的灯笼，说："哭和笑，都好看！"

Let's think

1 Recall the story. Find and circle the mistakes in the pictures.

2 Role-play as the people in the pictures with your friend and say.

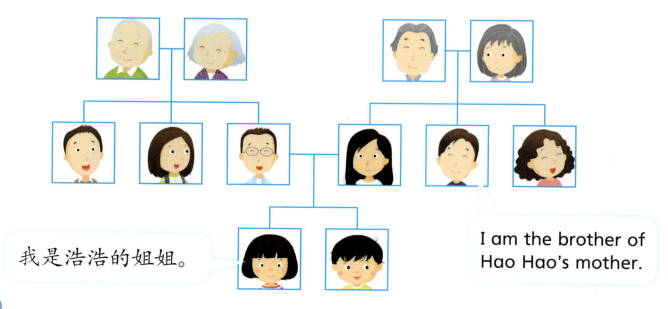

我是浩浩的姐姐。

I am the brother of Hao Hao's mother.

New words

1. Learn the new words.

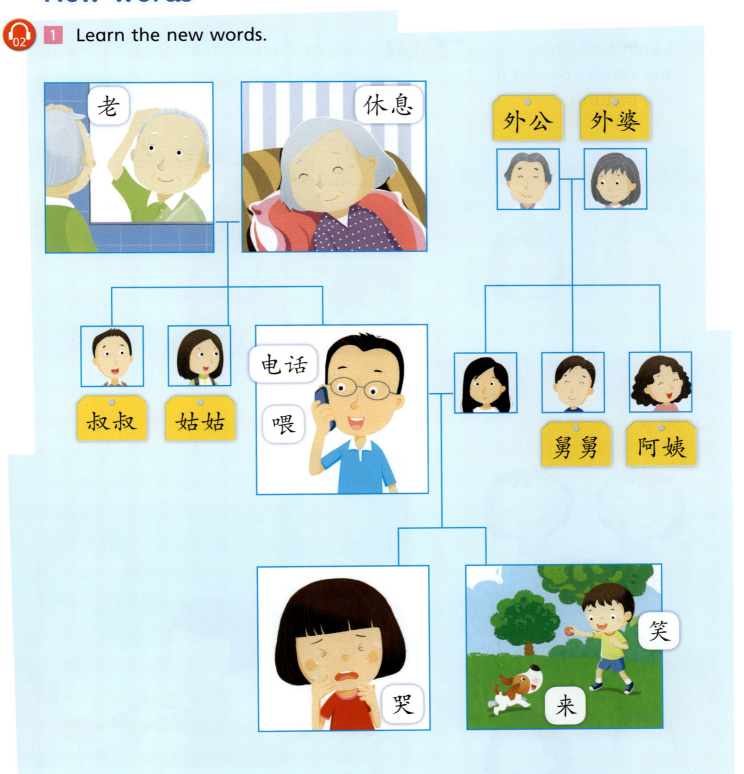

2. Listen to your teacher and point to the correct words above.

听听说说 Listen and say

1 Listen and circle the correct person in the pictures.

1 浩浩和谁去了动物园？

2 她最喜欢做什么？

3 浩浩给谁打电话？

2 Look at the pictures. Listen to the story a

玲玲，你怎么哭了？

我来了。我们一起做。

你看，玲玲笑了。

外婆，你来看看，我不会做这个。

你外公要多休息，他有点老了。

外公、外婆，谢谢你们！

3 Write the letters. Role-play with your friend.

a 休息　b 外公　c 来

喂，外婆你好。

喂，玲玲吗？

是的，外婆。明天你＿＿我家吗？

我明天去。

＿＿呢？

他不去，他在家＿＿。

Task

Ask your friend to role-play as your grandparent. Make a phone call to invite them and other relatives to a family gathering.

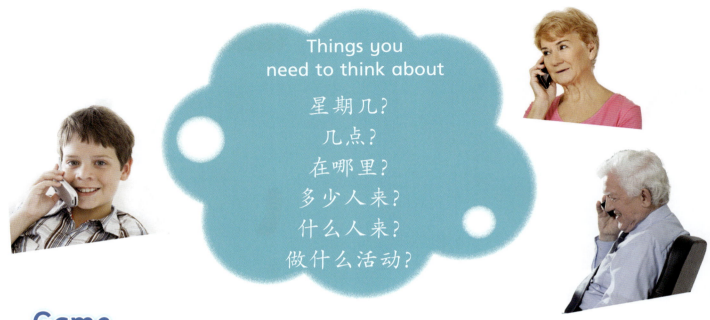

Things you need to think about

星期几？
几点？
在哪里？
多少人来？
什么人来？
做什么活动？

Game

Colour the female family members red and the male family members blue. Then say who they are to your friend.

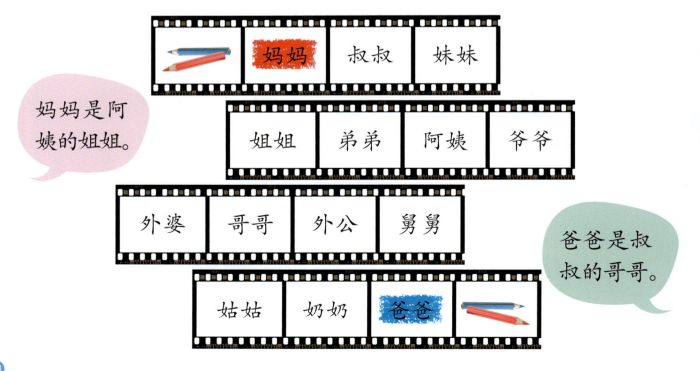

妈妈是阿姨的姐姐。

爸爸是叔叔的哥哥。

Chant

 Listen and say.

喂喂喂，喂喂喂，
请问你是谁？

舅舅好、阿姨好，
我是浩浩。

外公、外婆在家吗？
外公、外婆休息了。

再见舅舅，再见阿姨。
再见浩浩，再见浩浩。

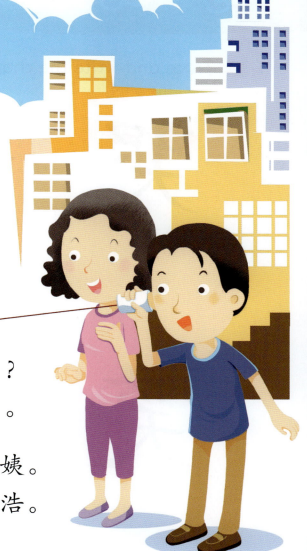

生活用语 Daily expressions

HAPPY HOLIDAYS

节日快乐！
Happy holidays!

TAKE A REST

休息休息。
Take a rest.

1 Trace and write the characters.

丶 丨 冂 冂 吅 吅 吧 哭 哭

丿 𠂉 ⺮ ⺮ ⺮ 笻 笻 笑

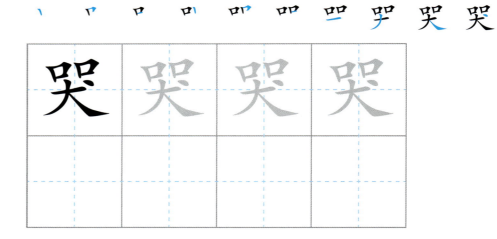

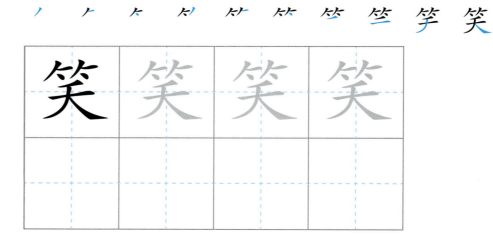

2 Write and say.

他___了。___很小。

她的脸圆圆的，她喜欢___。

3 Fill in the blanks with the correct words. Colour the balloons using the same colours.

因为　生日　笑

昨天是我的_____，外公外婆来我家了。我们唱_____歌，吃_____蛋糕。

_____我大了一岁，我很高兴，大家也很高兴，我们都___了。

拼音输入法 Pinyin input

Circle the correct numbers to type 'good morning'.

One of the phonetic-based input methods is Pinyin input. When typing a character, first type the Pinyin, and then the number for the character you need.

zao

1 早　2 造　3 遭　4 枣　5 燥　6 灶　7 糟　8 凿　9 躁　◀ ▶

shang

1 上　2 商　3 尚　4 伤　5 赏　6 裳　7 觞　8 殇　9 熵　◀ ▶

hao

1 好　2 号　3 浩　4 豪　5 郝　6 耗　7 昊　8 镐　9 蚝　◀ ▶

Cultures

Have you heard of the Mid-Autumn Festival? Learn about its traditions.

The Mid-Autumn Festival falls on the fifteenth day of the eighth month in the lunar calendar, in September or October in the Gregorian calendar.

Family and friends gather together to celebrate the unions and give thanks for the harvest.

The main traditions of the festival include eating mooncakes and lighting lanterns.

Project

1 Learn about some popular festivals in the world.

Christmas

We celebrate the birth of Jesus Christ.

New Year's Eve

People all over the world welcome the new year with fireworks.

Diwali

We worship the Hindu goddess of prosperity during this festival of lights.

Ramadan

For a month, we fast from sunrise to sunset to celebrate this Muslim festival.

2 Do some research on other festivals. Tell your friend about them.

我喜欢……
它在……日。
那天我……

我喜欢中国新年，因为有很多糖果。

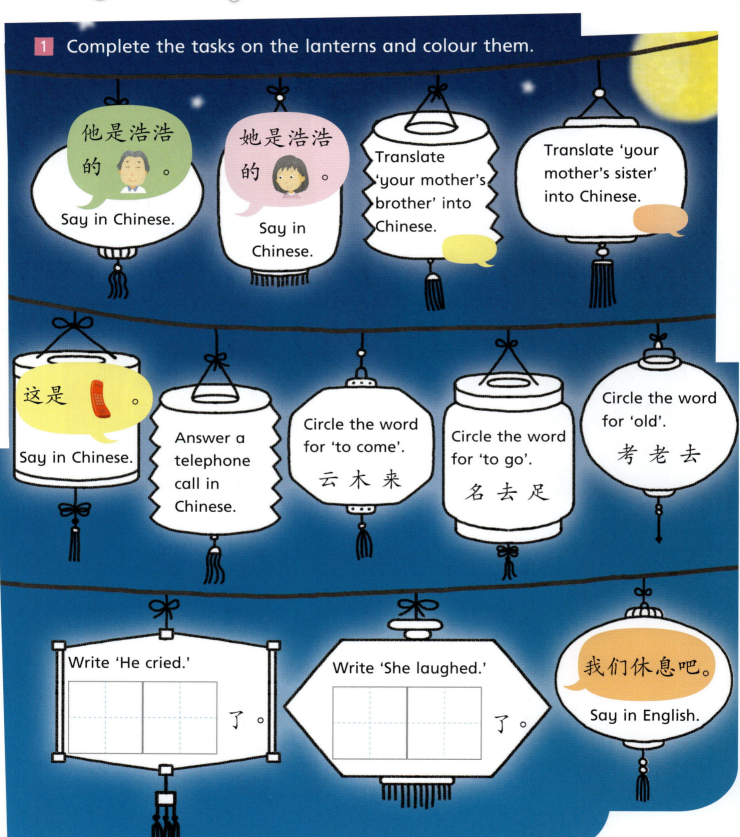

2 Work with your friend. Colour the stars and the chillies.

Words	说	读	写
外公	☆	☆	🌶
外婆	☆	☆	🌶
来	☆	☆	🌶
休息	☆	☆	🌶
老	☆	☆	🌶
哭	☆	☆	☆
笑	☆	☆	☆
舅舅	☆	🌶	🌶
阿姨	☆	🌶	🌶

Words and sentences	说	读	写
叔叔	☆	🌶	🌶
姑姑	☆	🌶	🌶
电话	☆	🌶	🌶
喂	☆	🌶	🌶
舅舅和阿姨也来了。	☆	🌶	🌶
叔叔和姑姑没来。	☆	🌶	🌶

Address extended family members	☆

3 What does your teacher say?

My teacher says ...

分享 Sharing

Words I remember

外公	wài gōng	mother's father
外婆	wài pó	mother's mother
来	lái	to come
休息	xiū xi	to rest
老	lǎo	old
哭	kū	to cry
笑	xiào	to laugh
舅舅	jiù jiu	mother's brother
阿姨	ā yí	mother's sister
叔叔	shū shu	father's younger brother
姑姑	gū gu	father's sister
电话	diàn huà	telephone
喂	wèi	hello (when answering the phone)

Other words

中秋节	zhōng qiū jié	Mid-Autumn Festival
月饼	yuè bǐng	moon cake
天上	tiān shàng	sky
月亮	yuè liang	moon
旅行	lǚ xíng	to travel
打	dǎ	to dial
老人	lǎo rén	old people
要	yào	to need
点	diǎn	a little
大人	dà rén	adult
灯笼	dēng long	lantern

Oxford University Press is a department of the University of Oxford.
It furthers the University's objective of excellence in research, scholarship,
and education by publishing worldwide. Oxford is a registered trade mark of
Oxford University Press in the UK and in certain other countries

Published in Hong Kong by
Oxford University Press (China) Limited
39th Floor, One Kowloon, 1 Wang Yuen Street, Kowloon Bay,
Hong Kong

© Oxford University Press (China) Limited 2017

The moral rights of the author have been asserted

First Edition published in 2017

All rights reserved. No part of this publication may be reproduced, stored in a
retrieval system, or transmitted, in any form or by any means, without the prior
permission in writing of Oxford University Press (China) Limited, or as expressly
permitted by law, by licence, or under terms agreed with the appropriate
reprographics rights organization. Enquiries concerning reproduction outside
the scope of the above should be sent to the Rights Department, Oxford
University Press (China) Limited, at the address above

You must not circulate this work in any other form
and you must impose this same condition on any acquirer

Illustrated by Anne Lee, KK Ng, KY Chan and Wildman

Photographs for reproduction permitted by Dreamstime.com

China National Publications Import & Export (Group) Corporation is an authorized distributor of
Oxford Elementary Chinese.

Please contact content@cnpiec.com.cn or 86-10-65856782

ISBN: 978019-942995-0

10 9 8 7 6 5 4 3 2